On Life and Death

Aristotle's Inquiry into the Nature of Existence

A Modern Translation

Adapted for the Contemporary Reader

Aristotle

Translated by Tim Zengerink

Table of Contents

PREFACE

MESSAGE TO THE READER

Dear Reader,

Thank you for choosing this edition; it is more than just a book—you are reading a living thread of humanity's literary heritage.

We'd like to invite you to **gain immediate, unlimited digital & audiobook access** to hundreds of the most treasured literary classics ever written—along with the option to **secure deluxe paperback, hardcover & box set editions at printing cost**. Together, we can **spark a new global literary renaissance** alongside our small, independent publishing house called "The Library of Alexandria."

Thousands of years ago, the Library of Alexandria stood as a beacon of knowledge—until it was lost to history. We aim to reignite that spirit of preservation and discovery right now, in the modern age—only this time, it's accessible to all, in every language and every format.

Picture a world where every timeless classic, novel, poem, or philosophical treatise is not only available to read but also updated for today's readers—modernized, translated into any language or dialect, and ready to enjoy in any format you choose, whether that is in an eBook, audiobook, paperback, or deluxe hardcover & box set version a printing cost.

By joining our movement to **rebuild the modern Library of Alexandria**, you become part of an unprecedented mission to offer:

- **Unlimited Audiobook & eBook Access to the Greatest Classics of All Time**

  Instantly explore thousands of legendary works, from Plato and Shakespeare to Jane Austen and Leo Tolstoy. All are instantly ready to read or listen to, giving you a complete literary universe at your fingertips.

- **Paperback & Deluxe Editions at Printing Costs:**

  Purchase any title in a paperback, deluxe hardbound, or deluxe boxset edition at printing costs, shipped right to your doorstep. Curate your personal library of Alexandria with editions worthy of display—crafted to last, designed to captivate, and delivered straight to your door.

- **Modern translations for Contemporary Readers in all languages and dialects**

  Discover a vast selection of classics reimagined in clear, current language—no more struggling with outdated phrases or obscure references. Next to the original versions, we aim to offer translations in as many languages and dialects as possible.

As we continue our translation efforts and add new languages, readers everywhere can connect with these works as if they were written today. *By bridging linguistic divides, you're contributing to ensuring that these timeless stories become more meaningful, accessible, and inspiring for people across the globe.*

• **Your Personal Library of Alexandria:**

Over the months and years, you'll curate a unique physical archive of classics—each volume a testament to your taste, curiosity, and love of knowledge. It's not just about owning books—it's about curating a cultural legacy you'll cherish and pass down for generations to come.

• **Join a Global Literary Renaissance:**

Your support fuels an ongoing mission: allowing us to reinvest in offering deluxe print editions (including special boxsets) at their true cost, broaden the range of available formats and translations, and extend the reach of these works to new audiences worldwide. By joining today, you're not just preserving a legacy of masterpieces; *you set in motion a powerful wave of literary accessibility.*

We are more than a publisher—we're a movement, and we can't do it alone. Your support lets us scale our mission, preserving and reimagining history's greatest works for tomorrow's readers.

Become a Torchbearer of knowledge.

Thank you for picking up this book and allowing us into your literary journey. As you turn the pages, know that you're part of something larger: a global effort to keep these stories alive, share their wisdom across borders and generations, and spark a true cultural revival for the modern era.

If this resonates with you—please consider taking the next step. By visiting:
www.libraryofalexandria.com

With gratitude and a shared love of knowledge,

The Modern Library of Alexandria Team

Visit:

www.libraryofalexandria.com

Or scan the code below:

Introduction

Ancient Greece was a civilization famous for its great contributions to philosophy, politics, art, and science. It thrived from the 8th century BCE until the Roman Empire started to decline. Greece's city-states, especially Athens, were the heart of culture and intellectual thought. This was the time when democracy began, impressive buildings like the Parthenon were built, and famous playwrights like Sophocles and Euripides produced their works. The Greeks' curiosity about the world around them laid the foundation for Western philosophy. Thinkers like Socrates, Plato, and later Aristotle, pushed the limits of what people understood about the world.

Greek society was deeply connected to theism, which focused on a large group of gods and goddesses who were believed to control every part of life. But this system did not prevent people from exploring new ideas. In fact, it coexisted with a growing interest in finding logical explanations for nature and human life. Intellectuals would often debate and discuss these ideas in public places like the Agora. Aristotle grew up in this dynamic environment, learning from earlier philosophers, and later challenging and expanding their ideas.

Aristotle's Life

Aristotle was born in 384 BCE in a small town called Stagira, located in northern Greece. His father, Nicomachus, was a doctor for King Amyntas of Macedon, and this allowed Aristotle to be around the Macedonian royal court from a young age. When his parents passed away, Aristotle was sent to Athens at the age of 17 to pursue his education. Athens was the center of intellectual life in Greece, and Aristotle joined Plato's Academy, which was the most respected school of the time. The Academy was a place where students discussed everything from ethics to science. Although Aristotle learned a lot from Plato, he did not always agree with him, especially when it came to metaphysics, which deals with the nature of reality.

After spending almost 20 years at the Academy, Aristotle left Athens around 347 BCE after Plato's death. He traveled around different cities in Greece, continuing to study and learn. In 343 BCE, he was invited to the court of King Philip II of Macedon, where he became the tutor of Philip's son, Alexander, who would later become known as Alexander the Great. Aristotle taught Alexander about philosophy, ethics, politics, and science. Aristotle's influence is visible in Alexander's leadership style, which showed respect for knowledge and strategic thinking.

After teaching Alexander, Aristotle returned to Athens in 335 BCE, where he opened his own school called the Lyceum. Unlike Plato's Academy, the Lyceum focused more on recording knowledge and observing nature. Aristotle and his students performed research, studied animals, and took notes on what they observed. The Lyceum became a major center of learning, and it rivaled Plato's Academy. This is also where Aristotle wrote many of his famous works.

Later in life, after the death of Alexander in 323 BCE, the political climate in Athens became difficult for Aristotle because of his connections to the Macedonian court. Accused of disrespecting the gods, Aristotle decided to leave Athens. He fled to Chalcis, where he passed away in 322 BCE. Even though he had to leave Athens, his legacy lived on through his many writings and the influence of his school, the Lyceum.

Aristotle's Impact on Western Thought

No figure looms larger over the development of Western philosophy and science than Aristotle. A student of Plato and tutor to Alexander the Great, he unified logic, ethics, politics, rhetoric, and metaphysics into a coherent system that shaped intellectual inquiry for centuries. Although his writings reflect the best knowledge of his era, they also reveal a distinctive way of understanding the world—one that balances observation with rigorous logical analysis. Over time, this method has profoundly influenced everything from political theory to modern scientific methodology.

Aristotle approached knowledge as an interconnected whole, seeing each field of study as a vital path toward truth. While many earlier thinkers focused on abstract concepts, he emphasized direct observation of the natural world. By systematically examining and classifying what he saw, Aristotle laid the groundwork for the empirical methods now central to modern science. Although our understanding of nature has evolved, his legacy endures in today's emphasis on evidence-based research.

Logic: The Foundation of Rational Inquiry

Often hailed as the "father of formal logic," Aristotle introduced a system of reasoning that shaped intellectual discourse for over two millennia. In works like the Organon, he analyzed how valid conclusions are drawn from premises and introduced syllogisms—deductive arguments that became standard tools in philosophy, theology, and science. Even contemporary logic, despite its modern mathematical and symbolic advancements, can trace many of its core principles back to Aristotle's pioneering analyses.

Metaphysics: Exploring the Nature of Reality

Aristotle's Metaphysics offered one of the earliest comprehensive explorations of existence at its most fundamental level. There, he described the nature of "being qua being" and introduced the concepts of potentiality and actuality to explain how things change and develop. These ideas deeply influenced medieval scholastics—both Christian and Islamic— who integrated Aristotelian reasoning into their theological frameworks. Today, discussions about consciousness, identity, and free will still reference these Aristotelian notions.

Ethics and the Pursuit of the Good Life

In the Nicomachean Ethics, Aristotle proposed that the ultimate aim of human life is eudaimonia, often translated as "happiness" or "flourishing." He argued that we achieve this through virtue, developed by cultivating good habits guided by reason. His famous Doctrine of the Mean asserts that moral virtue resides between two extremes—for instance, courage lies between recklessness and cowardice. This focus on character formation has profoundly shaped the tradition known as "virtue ethics," influencing modern debates on moral education, personal development, and what it means to live well.

Politics: The Role of the Individual in the City-State

Aristotle's practical approach to ethics naturally extended into political theory. In Politics, he explored various forms of government—monarchy, aristocracy, oligarchy, democracy—and weighed their merits and pitfalls. For Aristotle, a well-ordered polis (city-state) exists not merely for survival or trade but to enable its citizens to live virtuous, fulfilling lives. His conviction that ethics and politics are intertwined remains influential, informing contemporary discussions on citizenship, governance, and justice.

Rhetoric: The Art of Persuasion

In his treatise Rhetoric, Aristotle examined how persuasion works, detailing how arguments must appeal to ethos (credibility), pathos (emotion), and logos (logic). This clear framework for effective communication continues to guide public speakers, legal advocates, and writers. From ancient courtroom orations to modern political campaigns, Aristotelian rhetoric underpins many of the strategies people use to sway audiences and shape public opinion.

Beyond these core subjects, Aristotle made significant contributions to biology, physics, psychology, and aesthetics. In the Poetics, for example, he investigated why humans respond so powerfully to tragic drama, pioneering the concept of catharsis— the emotional release that audiences feel through art. Throughout the medieval period, thinkers like Thomas Aquinas integrated Aristotle's theories into Christian theology, while Islamic philosophers such as Avicenna and Averroes preserved, interpreted, and expanded upon his works.

Across centuries of reinterpretation and debate, Aristotle remains a living voice in contemporary thought. His insistence on systematically gathering evidence and connecting it to logical principles laid the foundation for what we now recognize as the scientific method. His inquiries into human flourishing, civic responsibility, and the nature of argument continue to spark discussion and inspire new research. From personal ethics to societal organization, Aristotle's ideas help us frame enduring questions about how best to live, learn, and understand reality.

In sum, Aristotle stands as a foundational pillar of Western thought. He bridged abstract theorizing and practical inquiry, bequeathing a vision of knowledge that values both reason and experience. From ethics and politics to science and art, his ideas have been woven into countless intellectual traditions. Even today, as we grapple with questions of morality, governance, and truth, we walk in the footsteps of an ancient thinker whose breadth of insight and depth of analysis continue to guide our pursuit of wisdom.

Final Thoughts

By preserving Aristotle's legacy, we protect the intellectual depth and rigor that defined his way of understanding the world. His systematic way of asking questions, his classification of knowledge, and his ethical theories are still relevant today, providing a model for critical thinking across many subjects. This preservation is important not just for philosophy students but for anyone interested in the foundations of human thought and the development of ideas that shape the world we live in.

One of the difficulties in studying Aristotle's work is that his ideas and language are complex. Translating these works into our modern language is a key step in making his profound insights easier for more people to understand. By putting his ideas into today's language, more readers can engage with his thoughts, even if they don't have a background in classical studies. Making Aristotle's work accessible means adapting them to modern ways of thinking without losing their original depth. This helps bridge the gap between ancient and modern readers, making sure Aristotle's work stays relevant.

Section 1

We now need to talk about youth, old age, life, and death. We will probably also need to explain the causes of breathing, since living and dying sometimes depend on it.

We have already explained the soul in detail elsewhere, and while it's clear that the soul itself isn't a physical thing, it must still exist in some part of the body that controls the other parts. Let's leave aside the other parts or abilities of the soul for now. When it comes to being an animal and being alive, we find that in all creatures that are both alive and animals, there is a single part that makes them both alive and animals. An animal cannot be an animal without being alive. However, something can be alive without being an animal, like plants, which live without feeling anything. It's through sensation that we tell the difference between animals and non-animals.

So, this part of the body that allows for life and being an animal must be the same in number but have different roles, because being alive and being an animal are not exactly the same thing. The organs of the different senses all connect to a single organ where all the senses meet when they work. This organ is located in the middle of the body, between what we call the front and the back (the front is where the senses come in, and the back is the opposite). Also, in all living things, the body is divided into upper and lower parts (even plants have upper and lower parts). This means the part of the body responsible for nutrition must be in the middle of these regions. We call the part where food comes in "the upper part" when we think of it by itself and not compared to the rest of the universe. The "lower part" is where waste is released.

Plants are the opposite of animals in this way. Humans, in particular, because of our upright posture, have our upper parts pointing upwards, like how the universe is structured. Other animals have their upper parts in a middle position. But in plants, because they are rooted in the ground and get their food from the soil, their upper part is always down. The roots of a plant are like the mouth of an animal, as this is where they take in food, whether it's from the earth or from another living thing.

All fully developed animals are divided into three parts: the part that takes in food, the part that releases waste, and the part that is in between. In larger animals, this middle part is called the chest, and in smaller animals, it's something similar. In some animals, this part is more clearly defined than in others. All animals that can move have extra body parts to help with this, such as legs or feet, which allow them to carry their whole body.

It's clear from both observation and reasoning that the source of the body's nourishment is in the middle of these three parts. Many animals can stay alive even when the head or the food container is cut off, as long as the middle part remains attached. This happens in many insects, like wasps and bees. Many other animals, besides insects, can also live after being cut in half as long as the part connected to nutrition remains.

While this middle part of the body is actually one organ, it has the potential to be multiple. These animals are similar to plants in this way. If you cut a plant into sections, each part can keep living, and you can grow multiple trees from one original plant. We will explain later why some plants can't survive when divided, while others can grow from cuttings. But in this way, plants and insects are alike.

The part of the body responsible for nourishment is actually one but has the potential to be many. This is also true for the part responsible for sensation, because the divided parts of these animals can still feel things. However, they can't maintain their structure like plants can because they don't have the organs needed to keep living. Some don't have the ability to grab food, while others can't digest it. They might also be missing other organs.

Animals that can be divided are like several animals growing together, but animals that are more complex are different because their bodies are united in the best possible way. This is why some organs, when divided, still show some sensation because they keep some life in them. For example, tortoises can keep moving even after their heart has been removed.

The same thing happens in both plants and animals. In plants, we see this when they grow from seeds, grafts, and cuttings. Growth from seeds always starts in the middle. All seeds have two halves, and the place where they join is where they attach to the plant, which is a middle part between the two sides. This middle part is where both the root and stem grow. So, the starting point is in the middle between the two. This is especially true for grafts and cuttings, which start growing from buds. The bud is the starting point of the branch and is located in the middle. When we graft a new plant or make a cutting, we either cut the bud or insert the new shoot into it because this is where new growth begins. This shows that growth starts in the middle, between the stem and the root.

In animals with blood, the heart is the first organ to develop. We know this from observing animals when possible. So, in animals without blood, the organ that is like the heart must also develop first. We've already said in our work on animal parts that veins come from the heart, and in animals with blood, the blood is the final nourishment that forms the body parts. This shows that the mouth plays one role in nutrition, and the stomach plays another, but the heart is in control and completes the process. So, in animals with blood, the source of both sensation and nutrition must be in the heart, because the other organs involved in nutrition only help the heart in its work. The main organ is responsible for completing the process, just like how a doctor's goal is to bring about health, not just to focus on smaller tasks.

In all animals with blood, the main organ for sensation is the heart, because this is where the common center for all the senses is located. This is clear for taste and touch because they can be directly connected to the heart. So, the other senses must also lead to the heart, since the heart is where changes start in the other sense organs, while the senses in the head, like taste and touch, are not connected to the heart. Also, if life is always located in the heart, then the source of sensation must also be there. An animal is called "alive" because it can sense things, and we call something an animal because it can feel. In other works, we've explained why some of the senses are connected to the heart and others are in the head. (This is why some people think that sensation comes from the brain.)

If we look at the facts, it's clear that the source of the sensitive soul, along with the part responsible for growth and nutrition, is located in the heart, which is in the middle of the body. This also makes sense from reasoning. In every case, Nature always chooses the best outcome when possible. If both the sensitive and the nutritive principles are located in the middle of the body, the parts responsible for processing food and the parts that receive food will work best. This is because the soul will be close to both, and the central position it holds is the place of control.

The thing that uses a tool and the tool itself must be different. If possible, they should also be separate in space, just like a flute and the hand that plays it. So, if an animal is defined by its ability to sense, this ability must be located in the heart in animals with blood, and in a similar part in animals without blood. In all animals, the body and its parts have some natural warmth, which is why they are warm when alive and cold when dead. This warmth must come from the heart in animals with blood, and from a similar organ in animals without blood. While all parts of the body use their natural heat to process food, the main organ plays the biggest role in this process. This is why life continues even when other parts of the body become cold. But when the warmth in this main organ is gone, death always follows because the heat in all the other parts depends on this organ. The soul is like a fire in this part of the body, which is the heart in animals with blood, and a similar organ in animals without blood. So, life depends on maintaining this heat, and death happens when this heat is destroyed.

It's important to note that fire can stop burning in two ways: either it goes out on its own or something else puts it out. When it stops by itself, we call it exhaustion, and when something else puts it out, we call it extinction. Fire can go out either way from the same cause. When there isn't enough fuel and the heat can't keep burning, the fire dies out. This happens because something blocks digestion and stops the fire from being fed. In other cases, the fire burns out from exhaustion—when heat builds up too much because there's no way to cool down or breathe. In this situation, the heat quickly uses up all its fuel before more can come in. This is why a small fire can be put out by a bigger one, and a candle flame gets swallowed up when placed in a large fire, just like any other burnable material. The bigger fire uses up the fuel before more can be added. Fire is always being created and moving forward, like a river, but it happens so fast we don't notice.

So, if the body's heat needs to be kept steady (which it does to stay alive), there has to be a way to cool down the source of heat. Think of what happens when you cover hot coals in a container. If they stay covered for too long, they burn out. But if you keep lifting the lid and putting it back down quickly, the coals will stay hot for a long time. Piling ashes on a fire also keeps it going, because ashes are porous and allow air to pass through, while also keeping the heat from escaping into the surrounding air. In our work *The Problems*, we've explained why covering a fire makes it go out, while piling ashes on it keeps it burning for a long time.

Everything that is alive has a soul, and as we've said, the soul can't exist without heat in the body. In plants, the natural heat is kept alive by the food they take in and the air around them. Food cools the body when it first enters, just like in humans. When a plant doesn't get food, it produces heat and becomes thirsty. Air, if it doesn't move, becomes hot, but when food enters, it causes movement, which continues until digestion is done, and this cools the body. If the air around the plant is too cold because of the season, the plant withers. Or if, in the heat of summer, the moisture from the ground can't cool the plant, the heat in the plant burns out. When this happens, we say the plants are scorched or burned by the sun. That's why people sometimes put stones or pots of water under the roots of plants to keep them cool.

Some animals live in water, while others live in the air. These environments provide the cooling they need—water for the ones in water, and air for those in the air. We will need to explain more about how exactly this cooling happens.

A few of the early philosophers talked about breathing. But they either didn't explain why animals breathe, or they gave incorrect explanations, showing they didn't know the facts very well. They also wrongly said that all animals breathe, which isn't true. So, we need to address these points first so we don't seem like we're criticizing those who are no longer alive without reason.

First, it's clear that all animals with lungs breathe. But in some animals, the lungs don't have much blood and are more like sponges, so they don't need to breathe as much. These animals can stay underwater for a long time, relative to their strength. All egg-laying animals, like frogs, have lungs like sponges. Tortoises can also stay underwater for a long time because their lungs don't hold much blood and don't produce much heat. Once their lungs fill with air, the movement of the lungs cools the animal and allows it to stay underwater for a while. However, if an animal holds its breath for too long, it will suffocate, because none of these animals can take in water the way fish do. On the other hand, animals with lungs full of blood need to breathe more because they have more heat. Animals without lungs don't breathe at all.

Democritus and others who wrote about breathing didn't say much about animals without lungs, but they seemed to think that all animals breathe. Anaxagoras and Diogenes both said that all animals breathe, and they tried to explain how fish and oysters breathe. Anaxagoras said that when fish push water through their gills, air forms in their mouths, because there can't be a vacuum. He thought they breathe by taking in this air. Diogenes said that when fish push water out through their gills, they suck air from the water into their mouths because a vacuum is formed in the mouth. He believed there was air in the water.

But these ideas don't work. They only describe part of what's going on and leave out the rest. Breathing involves both inhaling and exhaling air, but these explanations don't say anything about how these animals breathe out. They can't explain it because these animals would have to breathe out through the same passage they breathe in. This would mean that they would have to take water into their mouths while breathing out at the same time. But the air and water would meet and block each other. When the animal pushes water out, it would also have to push out its breath through the mouth or gills. As a result, it would be breathing in and out at the same time, which is impossible. So, if breathing means both inhaling and exhaling air, and these animals can't breathe out, then they can't breathe at all.

Also, the idea that fish breathe by pulling air from the water with their mouths is impossible because they don't have lungs or windpipes. Instead, their stomachs are close to their mouths, so they would have to suck air into their stomachs. If that were true, other animals would do the same, but they don't. Fish also don't do this when they're out of the water, which is obvious. In animals that breathe, you can see movement in the part of the body that pulls in air, but fish don't show any movement in their stomachs, only in their gills. Their gills move both when they are in the water and when they are on land gasping for air. Also, when animals that breathe are drowned, they release air bubbles as the air is forced out, like when a tortoise or frog is held underwater. But this never happens with fish, no matter how we try, because they don't take in air from outside.

If fish really breathed by pulling in air from the water, people should be able to do the same when they are underwater. If fish pull in air through their mouths, why couldn't humans or other animals do that too? But since humans can't do it, neither can fish. Also, why do fish die in the air and gasp as if they are suffocating? It's not because they lack food, and Diogenes' explanation is ridiculous. He says fish die because they take in too much air when out of the water, but in water, they take in just the right amount. But if that were true, land animals should also be able to suffocate from breathing too much air. But that doesn't happen. If all animals breathe, then insects must breathe too. Some insects, like centipedes, seem to live even after being cut into several pieces. How can they breathe when divided, and what organs do they use?

The reason these philosophers gave bad explanations is that they didn't understand the internal organs and didn't believe that everything in nature has a purpose. If they had asked what the purpose of breathing is and thought about the organs involved, like the lungs and gills, they would have figured it out sooner.

Democritus, however, did say that breathing has a purpose. He said it keeps the soul from being pushed out of the body. But he didn't say that nature designed breathing for this purpose. Like the other early philosophers, he didn't reach this level of understanding. He said the soul and heat are the same thing, made up of small, round particles. When the air around us presses on the body and tries to push the soul out, breathing helps prevent this. Democritus thought the air contains many particles of soul and mind, and when we breathe in, these particles enter the body and push back against the pressure, keeping the soul in place.

This is why, he said, life and death are connected to breathing in and out. Death happens when the pressure from the air around us becomes too strong, and the animal can no longer breathe in. At that point, the air can't get in to balance the pressure, and the soul is pushed out of the body. Death, according to him, is the result of the soul being forced out by the pressure of the air around us. Death happens naturally with old age, or unnaturally through violence.

But Democritus didn't explain why death happens or why everything must eventually die. He should have explained whether the cause of death is internal or external, especially since death happens at certain times in life and not others. He also didn't explain where breathing begins or whether its cause is internal or external. It's not true that the air outside controls breathing. The cause of breathing must come from within the body, not from pressure outside. It's also strange to think that the air around us would both squeeze the body and, by entering, expand it at the same time. This is Democritus' theory and how he explains it.

But if our earlier explanation is correct, and not all animals breathe, then Democritus' explanation of death applies only to animals that breathe, not to all animals. And even for animals that breathe, his explanation isn't correct, as we can see from experience. In hot weather, when we get warmer and need to breathe more, we breathe faster. But when the air around us is cold, it shrinks and tightens the body, which slows down breathing. At this time, the outside air should enter the body and cancel out the pressure, but the opposite happens. When we can't breathe out and the heat inside builds up too much, we need to breathe, which means we need to take in air. In hot weather, people breathe faster to cool down, even though Democritus' theory would suggest that they should be adding more heat to their bodies.

The idea from *Timaeus* about breathing, where air is pushed around in the body, doesn't explain how heat is kept in animals other than those that live on land. It also doesn't say if their heat comes from the same or a different source. If breathing only happens in land animals, we should be told why. If other animals also breathe but in a different way, then this form of breathing needs to be explained, assuming all animals breathe.

Also, the explanation seems made up. It says that when hot air leaves the mouth, it pushes the air around it, which then enters the body again through the pores of the skin, filling the place where the warm air came out. This happens because a vacuum (empty space) can't exist. Then, when the air heats up, it leaves the body again through the same route and pushes the warm air back inside through the mouth. They say this process happens continuously when we breathe in and out.

But with this explanation, it would mean we breathe out before we breathe in, which isn't true. The opposite is what really happens, as we can observe. Even though breathing in and out alternates, the last thing we do before death is exhale, so the first act must have been to inhale.

Also, those who explain breathing like this don't say why animals have this function. They make it sound like breathing just happens as part of being alive, but it clearly has control over life and death. When an animal can't breathe, it dies. It's also strange to suggest that the hot air leaving the body is easy to notice, but we can't detect the air entering the lungs and heating up again. It's even more ridiculous to think that breathing involves taking in heat when the opposite is true: we breathe out hot air and take in cool air. When it's hot, we pant because the air coming in isn't cooling us enough, so we have to breathe more frequently.

But we shouldn't think that breathing is for feeding the body like food. Breathing isn't about adding fuel to the body's internal fire, as some have said, with the air acting like food for the flame and then being breathed out. I'll repeat the argument I used earlier against this idea. If that were true, we would see the same thing happening in other animals since they all have body heat. Also, how could breathing create heat? We see that heat comes from food, not air. This theory would also mean that the same passage in the body would be used for taking in food and pushing out waste, but we don't see that happening in other cases.

Empedocles also explained breathing, but he didn't make clear what its purpose is or whether it's universal in all animals. He talked about breathing through the nostrils as if it were the main kind of breathing. But the air that enters through the nostrils also passes through the windpipe and out of the chest, and without the windpipe, the nostrils can't function. Also, if an animal can't breathe through its nose, it's fine. But if it can't breathe through its windpipe, it dies. Nature uses nose breathing for smelling in some animals. The reason why only some animals have it is that, while most animals can smell, they don't all have the same organs for it.

Empedocles also described how breathing works by saying that certain blood vessels hold blood but are not filled with it. These vessels have openings that connect to the air outside the body. The openings are small enough to keep the solid parts of the blood in but large enough for air to pass through. He said that when the blood moves down, air comes in, and this causes inhaling. When the blood moves up, air is pushed out, causing exhaling. He compared this to a water clock, a device used to measure time with water.

Here's how he explained it:

"All things breathe in and out. Their bodies have small tubes that reach the outer edges. These tubes have many channels leading through the nostrils. When the blood moves away, air rushes in. But when the blood moves up, air flows out. This is like a water clock. When a girl puts her hand over the tube and dips it in water, no water enters because the air is trapped. But when she lets the air escape, water rushes in. Just like the water clock, the blood moves, creating space for the air to flow in or out."

That's how he explained breathing. But as we've said, all animals that breathe do so through their windpipe, whether they breathe through their mouth or nose. If he's talking about this kind of breathing, we need to ask how it matches his explanation. The facts seem to go against it. The chest rises like a bellows when we inhale. It makes sense that heat would lift it up and that the blood would gather in the warm area. But the chest sinks back down when we exhale, just like a bellows. The difference is that in breathing, the air comes in and goes out through the same passage, while in a bellows, the air enters and exits through different places.

If Empedocles is only talking about breathing through the nose, he's mistaken. Nose breathing doesn't just involve the nostrils; it also passes through the area near the uvula, at the roof of the mouth. Some of the air goes through the nostrils, and some goes through the mouth, both when we breathe in and when we breathe out.

These are the problems with how other philosophers have explained breathing.

• • •

The End

The End

Thank you for Reading

Dear Reader,

We hope this timeless classic has sparked your imagination and enriched your literary journey. Now that you've turned the final page, we want to share a vision for the future of reading—one where every classic you've ever wanted to explore is at your fingertips, in a format that best suits your life.

We'd like to invite you to **gain immediate, unlimited digital & audiobook access** to hundreds of the most treasured literary classics ever written—along with the option to **secure deluxe paperback, hardcover & box set editions at printing cost**. Together, we can **spark a new global literary renaissance** alongside our small, independent publishing house called "The Library of Alexandria."

Thousands of years ago, the Library of Alexandria stood as a beacon of knowledge—until it was lost to history. We aim to reignite that spirit of preservation and discovery right now, in the modern age—only this time, it's accessible to all, in every language and every format.

Picture a world where every timeless classic, novel, poem, or philosophical treatise is not only available to read but also updated for today's readers—modernized, translated into any language or dialect, and ready to enjoy in any format you choose, whether that is in an eBook, audiobook, paperback, or deluxe hardcover & box set version a printing cost.

By joining our movement to **rebuild the modern Library of Alexandria**, you become part of an unprecedented mission to offer:

- **Unlimited Audiobook & eBook Access to the Greatest Classics of All Time**

  Instantly explore thousands of legendary works, from Plato and Shakespeare to Jane Austen and Leo Tolstoy. All are instantly ready to read or listen to, giving you a complete literary universe at your fingertips.

- **Paperback & Deluxe Editions at Printing Costs:**
  Purchase any title in a paperback, deluxe hardbound, or deluxe boxset edition at printing costs, shipped right to your doorstep. Curate your personal library of Alexandria with editions worthy of display—crafted to last, designed to captivate, and delivered straight to your door.

- **Modern translations for Contemporary Readers in all languages and dialects**

Discover a vast selection of classics reimagined in clear, current language—no more struggling with outdated phrases or obscure references. Next to the original versions, we aim to offer translations in as many languages and dialects as possible.

As we continue our translation efforts and add new languages, readers everywhere can connect with these works as if they were written today. *By bridging linguistic divides, you're contributing to ensuring that these timeless stories become more meaningful, accessible, and inspiring for people across the globe.*

- **Your Personal Library of Alexandria:**

Over the months and years, you'll curate a unique physical archive of classics—each volume a testament to your taste, curiosity, and love of knowledge. It's not just about owning books—it's about curating a cultural legacy you'll cherish and pass down for generations to come.

- **Join a Global Literary Renaissance:**

Your support fuels an ongoing mission: allowing us to reinvest in offering deluxe print editions (including special boxsets) at their true cost, broaden the range of available formats and translations, and extend the reach of these works to new audiences worldwide.

By joining today, you're not just preserving a legacy of masterpieces; *you set in motion a powerful wave of literary accessibility.*

We are more than a publisher—we're a movement, and we can't do it alone. Your support lets us scale our mission, preserving and reimagining history's greatest works for tomorrow's readers.

Become a Torchbearer of knowledge.

Thank you for picking up this book and allowing us into your literary journey. As you turn the pages, know that you're part of something larger: a global effort to keep these stories alive, share their wisdom across borders and generations, and spark a true cultural revival for the modern era.

If this resonates with you—please consider taking the next step. By visiting:
www.libraryofalexandria.com

With gratitude and a shared love of knowledge,

The Modern Library of Alexandria Team

Visit:

www.libraryofalexandria.com

Or scan the code below:

Visit

www.libraryofalexandria.com

Or scan the code below:

www.ingramcontent.com/pod-product-compliance
Lightning Source LLC
Chambersburg PA
CBHW012012290326
41934CB00017BA/3470